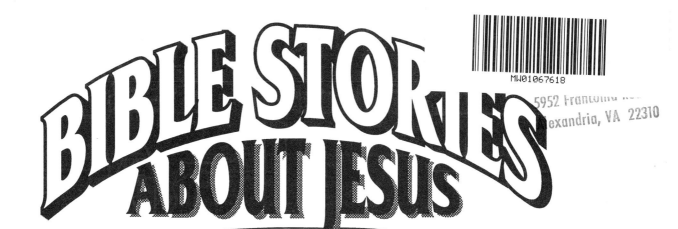

BIBLE STORIES ABOUT JESUS

Activities for Ages 2 & 3

Publisher	*Arthur L. Miley*
Author	*Darlene Hoffa*
Managing Editor	*Jack Cavanaugh*
Editorial Director	*Carol Rogers*
Art Director	*Deborah Birch*
Production Coordinator	*Valerie Fetrow*
Illustrator	*Roger Johnson*
Cover Design	*Court Patton*
Proofreader	*Heather Swindle*

Rainbow Books
Copyright 1998 • Seventh Printing
Rainbow Books • P.O. Box 261129 • San Diego, CA 92196

#RB36111
ISBN 0-937282-04-9

*Dedicated to Sherrol, Mary, and Jeanne, my daughters
and very best friends, who once learned by my side and
who now teach me.*

Darlene Hoffa

"Remember what Christ taught and let His words
enrich your lives and make you wise."

— Colossians 3:16 (TLB)

BIBLE STORIES ABOUT JESUS

Activities for Ages 2 & 3

Introduction

The best gift you can give children is to invite them to learn about Jesus. Jesus' life, translated from the Gospels on a child's level of understanding, can make an impact that lasts a lifetime. Even the smallest child can experience the wonder of Jesus' birth, the excitement of His childhood, the truths of His teachings, and the assurance of His death and resurrection.

Bible Stories About Jesus includes a wealth of activities suited for a variety of teaching situations. These creative Bible learning activities are based on 26 favorite Bible stories from the life of Jesus. All are created for the abilities of twos and threes — scribble coloring, making paper bag and stick puppets, sponge-painting, using play clay, playing active games, and even role-playing Gospel stories. Full-size patterns and figures are included, to ensure successful projects every time. Most activities require only ordinary school supplies or household items.

On each page, the name of the Gospel story and its Scripture reference are located beside a picture of the Bible, for easy reference. (Unless

otherwise noted, the King James Version of the Bible is used.) Each story is reinforced with two different Bible-learning activities, on facing pages. Either or both activities may be used to teach the story about Jesus. All activities are designed to supplement and enhance the teaching of the Gospel stories.

Each activity begins with two or three short paragraphs which introduce the story of Jesus and give step-by-step directions. These paragraphs may be read aloud to the children. The activity itself reinforces the story's message and relates the Bible truth to the child's life. Twos and threes will enjoy this hands-on approach to Jesus and His message.

The checklist indicates a special "For the Teacher" section, located at the bottom of each activity page. This paragraph contains addi-

tional instructions for the teacher, valuable teaching tips, and other ideas for using the activity. Place a sheet of paper over this section before duplicating the page, so it does not appear on the children's papers. Additional teaching activities and tips are included at the end of each chapter.

The activities in this book have been designed to be simple and easy to complete. The pages are perforated for easy removal. Materials should be used under the direction of an adult, and close supervision is recommended at all times. Care should be taken to protect the children from injury. Always keep staples, scissors, paper fasteners, and all other items which could cause possible harm out of the hands of twos and threes.

Children will look forward to and will eagerly take part in these creative activities. The wide variety of learning projects — over 52 in all — will help twos and threes learn and remember the stories of Jesus as they experience His love firsthand.

Outreach Idea

The chapter divisions following pages 6, 18, and 54 may be duplicated and used as promotional flyers. Replace "Activities for Ages 2 & 3" with your church or group name and write a "personal" note at the bottom of the page before duplicating. Fold the page in thirds, tape closed, address the back, add a stamp and a return address, and mail one to each child. Ask the children to color the pages and bring them to the first class session.

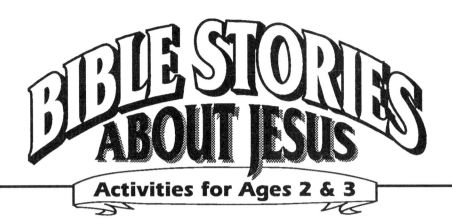

Activities for Ages 2 & 3

Table of Contents

BIBLE STORIES ABOUT JESUS

Activities for Ages 2 & 3

Jesus' Birth & Childhood

The Angel's Good News
Luke 1:26-38

One day God sent an angel to tell Mary some good news. God's Son, Jesus, was coming to earth as a baby. God had chosen Mary to be Jesus' mother. At first Mary was afraid, but then she was happy to obey God. The angel went back to heaven.

Moving Angel Picture

Color the picture of Mary's home and the angel. Your teacher will help you cut out the angel and tape it to a ribbon attached to the back of the picture. Make the angel come to tell Mary the good news and leave to go back to heaven.

Finished Picture

For the Teacher: Let the children color Mary and the angel. Cut the pictures apart. Help the children glue Mary onto a sheet of 6 x 9-inch construction paper. Tape the angel to one end of a 6-inch piece of stiff ribbon. Help them tape the other end of the ribbon to the back of the picture. Show the children how to make the angel come to bring Mary the good news and then go back to heaven. Talk about how God always helps us when we obey Him.

Good News Angel Puppet

The Angel's Good News
Luke 1:26-38

God sent an angel to tell Mary the good news that Jesus, God's Son, was coming. God told Mary that she would be Jesus' mother. Mary was glad to obey God.

You can obey God, too. You can tell the good news that Jesus is God's Son.

You can make an angel to help you tell the good news. Color the angel's hair and wings. Your teacher will help you cut them out and glue them on a paper sack to make a puppet. Your teacher also will help you give the angel a halo.

Apply glue here

Cut two wings

For the Teacher: Duplicate the angel pattern, one for each child. Let the children color the angels. Cut the face and mouth apart, and help the children glue them to the paper bag, as shown. Help them tape a chenille wire to the angel's back. Tape the halo on the other end of the chenille wire. Show the children how to make the angel say, "Jesus is God's Son."

A Special Baby Arrives
Luke 2:1-7

Room for Jesus Picture

When Jesus was born, all the hotels were filled with guests. But God had a plan for His son, Jesus. An innkeeper let Mary and Joseph use his stable. Mary wrapped Jesus in strips of cloth. Soft hay made a cozy pillow. A cow's manger made a crib for Baby Jesus.

Color the picture of Jesus' birth. Your teacher will help you glue doors onto the picture. You can open the doors and see the room where Jesus was born. God had a plan for Jesus, and God has a special plan for you, too.

Glue here

Glue here

Finished Picture

For the Teacher: Pre-cut two 4 1/4 x 9-inch pieces of brown construction paper for each child. After children color the picture, spread glue on the side margins. Give each child two pre-cut pieces of brown paper. Help them place the paper over the picture and press the edges onto the glue. Fold the doors back for easy opening. Show children how to open the doors and say, "God had a plan for Jesus. He has a special plan for me, too."

Blanket for Baby Jesus

Mary and Joseph were far from home when Jesus was born, but Mary had taken along warm blankets for her new baby. She wrapped Jesus in the blankets and put Him gently in the manger. You can make a blanket for Baby Jesus, too.

Color the picture. Your teacher will help you wrap the baby in the blanket and fasten it with a soft tie. Make Baby Jesus feel snug and safe. You can make a manger for Jesus. Sing Jesus your favorite song. Say, "Sleep well, Baby Jesus."

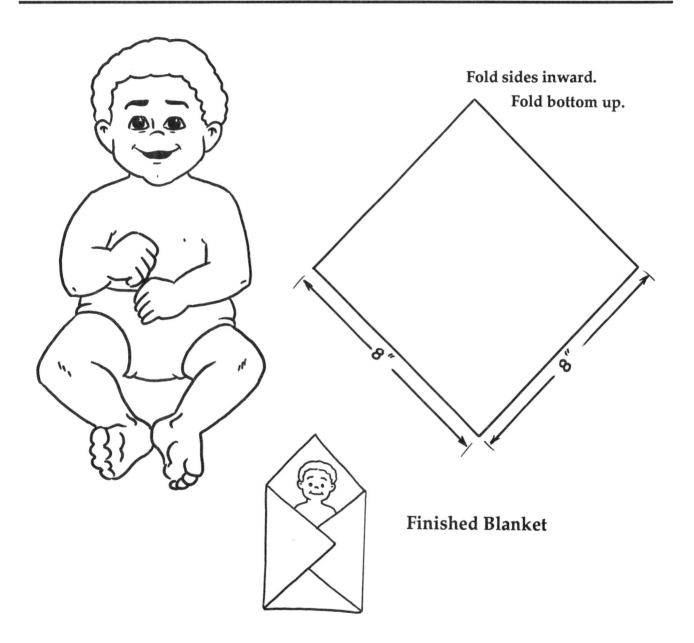

Fold sides inward.
Fold bottom up.

8"   8"

Finished Blanket

For the Teacher: Before class, cut an 8 x 8-inch square of flannel and four 9 x 12-inch strips of yellow paper for each child. After the children color, cut out their baby for them. Give each child a square of flannel and show them how to wrap Baby Jesus. You may tie a ribbon around the blanket in a bow. Give each child a small envelope to use as a manger. Help them fold the yellow strips and glue them in the manger for straw. Lay Jesus on top.

The Shepherd's Surprise
Luke 2:8-20

Popcorn Sheep Picture

One night shepherds were watching their sheep in a field. A bright light shone in the sky. The shepherds were afraid.

An angel told the shepherds not to be afraid. The angel explained that Jesus had been born. Jesus' birth was good news.

Color the shepherds. Your teacher will help you glue popcorn sheep on the hill and a bright light in the sky. You can take your picture home and tell your friends and family the story of the shepherds.

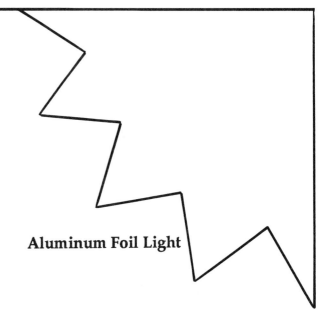

Aluminum Foil Light

Finished Picture

For the Teacher: Air pop popcorn before class. Pre-cut the lights from foil and the shepherds from white paper, one for each child. After they color the shepherds, give each child a 6 x 9-inch piece of black paper. Spread glue on the lower righthand corner, and show the children how to add popcorn to make a flock of sheep. Help them glue the bright light in the sky and the shepherd on the ground. Glue a chenille wire staff into the shepherd's hand.

Hurrying Shepherds

The shepherds were excited to hear that Jesus had been born. The shepherds hurried away to find Jesus in the manger. Then the shepherds hurried to tell others the good news that Jesus was born.

You can tell others that Jesus was born, too.

Color the shepherd and his feet. Your teacher will help you cut them out and attach the feet to the shepherd with a paper fastener. You can make the shepherd hurry to Baby Jesus and hurry to tell others the good news.

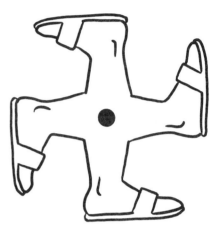

For the Teacher: Pre-cut the shepherd and feet pictures. Punch holes, as shown. Help the children put the feet in place by matching the holes. Attach the feet with a paper fastener. Do not let children hold the hole punch or paper fasteners. Put a piece of tape over the prongs of the paper fastener on the back of the shepherd. Help children glue terry cloth pieces on the shepherd's robe and tape a chenille wire to his hand for a staff.

13

Wise Men Look for Jesus
Matthew 2:1-11

Follow the Star Game

The wise men came a long way looking for Baby Jesus. God made a special star to show them where to go. The wise men followed the star until the star stopped over the place where Jesus lay. The wise men were very happy to find Baby Jesus.

You can make a wise man hat from construction paper. Your teacher will help you decorate your hat with colored foil and bright paper jewels. Then your teacher will show you how to play the Follow the Star Game.

For the Teacher: Pre-cut a star from gold paper and glue it to a strip of sturdy cardboard. Pre-cut crowns and 1 3/4 x 12-inch strips from purple construction paper, one crown and one strip for each child. Give children small, pre-cut squares of colored foil and bright paper to glue on their crowns. Staple a paper strip to one side of each crown. Place the crown around the child's head to size and staple the other end of the strip to the crown.

Gifts for Jesus Mobile

When the wise men found Jesus, they gave Him gifts and prayed to show Jesus that they loved Him. You can show Jesus you love Him, too. When you are kind and helpful, when you pray, and when you go to church you are showing Jesus you love Him.

Color the pictures the teacher has cut out for you. Your teacher will help you make a mobile to take home. You can hang the mobile in your room to remember ways to show that you love Jesus.

Finished Mobile

 For the Teacher: Pre-cut a double set of pictures for each child. After they finish coloring, give each child three pieces of bright yarn of varying lengths. Help them tape a piece of yarn to the back of a heart, a smiling face, and a church. Help the children glue the other set of pictures to the back of the matching pictures, as shown. Then help the children tape the ends of each piece of yarn to a plastic hanger to make a mobile.

Jesus Grows Up
Luke 2:41-52

Build a Church

One day Jesus went to church with Mary and Joseph. Many people went with Jesus and His family. Jesus liked to go to God's house.

Jesus enjoyed hearing the teachers and listening to God's Word. You can go to church and listen to God's Word, too.

You can make a church with doors on the outside and people on the inside. Your teacher will help you glue your church picture to a box. Then you can open the doors so that people can go in and out.

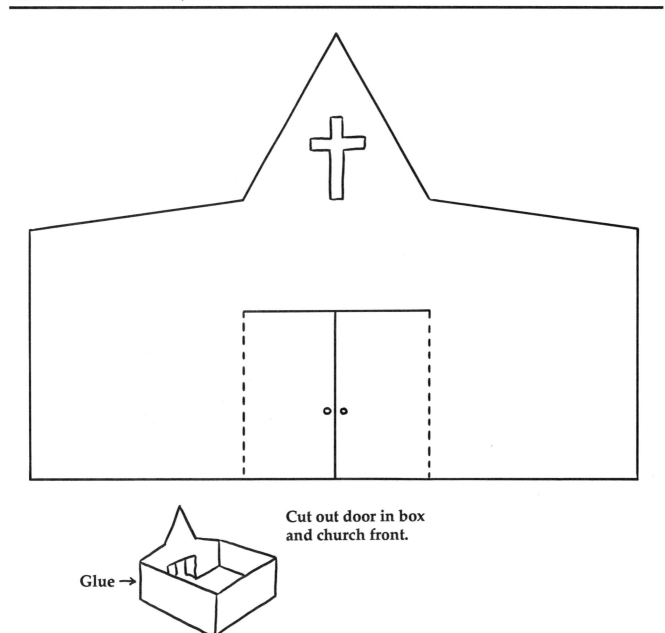

Cut out door in box and church front.

Glue →

For the Teacher: Duplicate the church picture onto sturdy white paper, one for each child. Cut the doors on the solid lines and fold open. Provide a small gift box or flavored gelatin box for each child's church. Pre-cut a small opening for the door. Help children glue the church pictures on the boxes. Talk about Jesus going to church with His parents. Talk about going to church today. Give children tiny graham cracker figures to go in and out of the church.

My Growing Up Book

Jesus was once a baby and then a child, just like you. He learned new things. He grew in many ways. He gradually got taller.

Jesus loved and obeyed God. He loved His family and friends. Jesus went to God's house to worship and pray.

You can make a Growing Up Book. Color the pictures. Your teacher will help you add a bright cover and tie your book with yarn. You can talk about the many ways you are growing, just like Jesus grew.

My Growing Up Book

I am learning new things.

3 YEARS
2 YEARS

I am growing taller.

I love God.

I love others.

For the Teacher: Pre-cut a cover of colorful 3 x 7-inch paper and a set of book pages from the pattern, one for each child. Punch holes in the cover and pages for the yarn, as shown. Do not let the children use the hole punch. After children color the pictures, help them string yarn through the pages and the cover and tie the yarn to make a book. Talk about the pages: learning new things, growing taller, loving God, and being a loving person.

TEACHING ACTIVITIES

Jesus' Birth & Childhood

The Angel's Good News (Pages 8 and 9)

Tell the Christmas story from Luke 1:26-38. Talk about the angel's good news for Mary.

Moving Angel Picture: Read the first paragraph to the children. After they finish their pictures, tell the story again. Prompt them to move the angel to Mary and then back to heaven as you tell the story.

Good News Angel Puppet: After children make their puppets, let them practice saying, "Jesus is God's Son." Then tell the story responsively. After each sentence or two, have the children use their puppets to say, "Jesus is God's Son." This will work best if you hold a puppet, too.

A Special Baby Arrives (Pages 10 and 11)

Describe the sights, sounds, and smells of a stable. Tell the Christmas story from Luke 2:1-7.

Play the Innkeeper Game. Have children stand in a line, side by side. Choose one child to be Joseph. The others are innkeepers. Place Joseph in front of the first innkeeper and help him ask, "Do you have room?" Move Joseph down the line, and prompt him to ask each innkeeper. All say "no," except the last one, who says, "yes." Joseph then moves to the end of the line and becomes the innkeeper who says yes. The first innkeeper becomes the next Joseph. Continue until each child has had a turn as Joseph.

The Shepherd's Surprise (Pages 12 and 13)

Tell the story of the shepherds from Luke 2:8-20. Talk about the duties of a shepherd. Explain that shepherds spent their time outside, finding food for their sheep and watching them graze. Describe their excitement when they heard of Jesus' birth.

Hurrying Shepherds: After the children finish their shepherds, tell the story again. Let them follow you with their shepherds as you hurry to Bethlehem, then hurry to tell others the good news, and then return, praising God.

Wise Men Look for Jesus (Pages 14 and 15)

Talk about what it means to be wise. Tell the story of the wise men from Matthew 2:1-11. Explain that the wise men gave Jesus gifts and prayed to show Jesus that they loved Him.

Follow the Star Game: After children make their crowns, help them put on their crowns and pretend to be wise men. Then play the Star Game. Hold the star, and lead the children around the room or play area, following the star to find Jesus. The children may take turns being the leader and holding the special star. This game could end at a manger scene or picture of Jesus.

Jesus Grows Up (Pages 16 and 17)

Help children understand that God's house is the church. Tell the story of Luke 2:41-52. Explain that as Jesus grew, He enjoyed going to God's house and listening to God's Word. As children grow, they can enjoy going to God's house, the church, and listening to God's Word.

My Growing Up Book: Enlarge a copy of each picture to make a 8 1/2 x 11-inch book. Color the pictures, and look at them with the children. After children make their books, "read" them together. Talk about ways that the children are growing as they look at each picture. Turn the pages in the large book, as children look at their own books.

BIBLE STORIES ABOUT JESUS

Activities for Ages 2 & 3

Jesus' Life & Ministry

Follow Me
Matthew 4:18-20

Follow Me Sandals

Jesus wanted helpers to tell God's good news. One day, as He walked beside the blue sea, Jesus invited Peter and Andrew to join Him. "Follow me," Jesus said, and they did.

Jesus' sandals left footprints in the thick dust. It was easy to follow the footprints.

You can make sandals to remember to follow Jesus. Your teacher will show you how to make sandal straps and ties to glue to your sandals. The sandals will help you remember that Jesus left us beautiful footprints to follow.

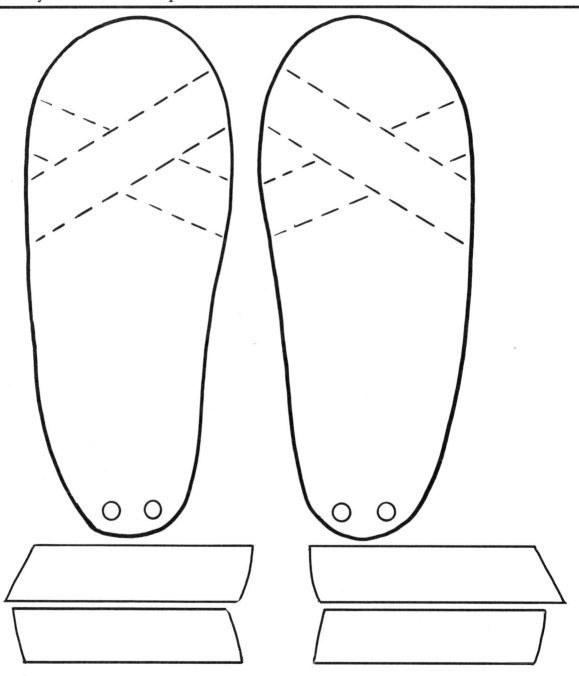

For the Teacher: Pre-cut the sandals out of bright poster board or paper. Let the children glue on straps of contrasting colored paper, as shown. Punch holes and add a ribbon tie for the sandals so they can hang in the child's room or on the refrigerator. Talk about ways we can follow Jesus. Lead the children in a game of Follow the Leader. Lead them in jumping, skipping or clapping. Talk about how happy we feel when we follow our leader, Jesus.

Whose Footprints Picture

Many living things leave footprints or tracks. God created each living thing with a special set of footprints. Ducks have different footprints than cats. Goats have different footprints than horses. People have different footprints than bears.

Can you tell whose footprints these are below? Look carefully at the pictures of living creatures. Then look at the footprints. Draw a line to connect the footprints with the correct living thing.

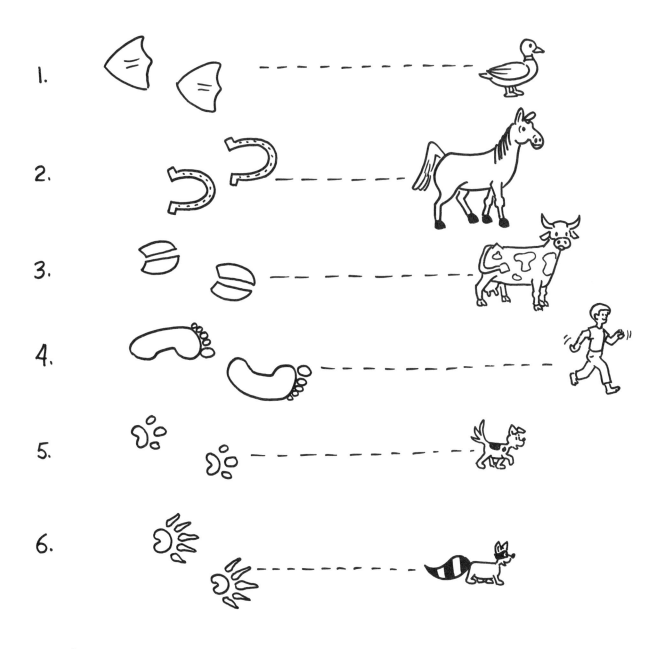

1.

2.

3.

4.

5.

6.

For the Teacher: Give each child a puzzle and a pencil or crayon. Talk about each set of footprints, and help the children draw a line to the living thing that might have made them. Talk about where we see footprints, such as in sand, thick carpet, and mud. Make learning cards, with the creature on the front and its footprint on the back. Show children the footprint and let them guess who made it.

The Lighted Candle
Matthew 5:14-16

Shining Bright Candle

Jesus said we can be like a lighted candle to show God's love to others. One way to show our love is to be kind to others. When we are kind, other people may want to know about God, too. What are some ways you can be kind to other people?

Your teacher will help you make a candle picture. Color the candle. You can add a bright glowing light. Your teacher will help you glue the light to your picture. The candle will remind you to be kind to others.

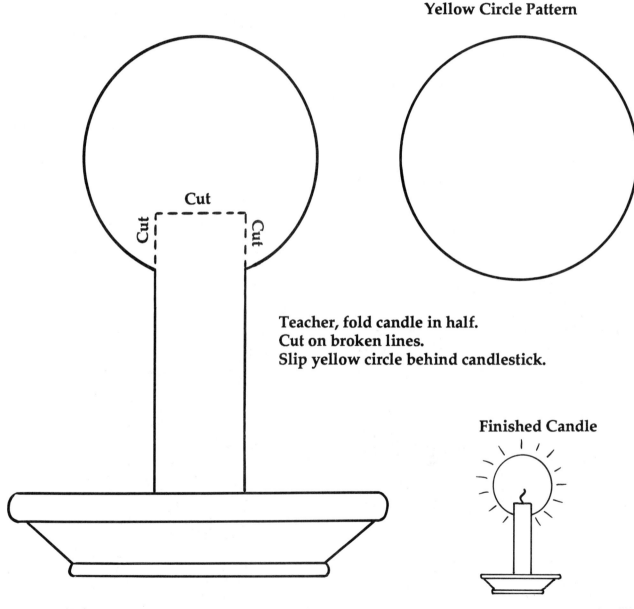

Yellow Circle Pattern

Cut

Cut   Cut

Teacher, fold candle in half.
Cut on broken lines.
Slip yellow circle behind candlestick.

Finished Candle

For the Teacher: Duplicate the candle picture and use the circle pattern to make a bright yellow circle for each child. After the children color the candle, fold it as shown and cut the candlestick on the broken lines. Help the children light the candle by slipping the yellow circle behind the candlestick and gluing or taping their candlelight in place. Help them glue a short piece of black yarn for the wick. Talk about ways that they can be kind and loving.

Helpful Lights Game

The Lighted Candle
Matthew 5:14-16

Many helpful lights remind us that we can help Jesus show God's love. Lights can make us feel safe or help us see better. Lights can help us look at picture books in a dark room. Lights keep us from falling when we are walking at night.

Can you name all the things that make light in the picture? Which of them do you use in your home? Which lights help you see outside? Color the pictures. Mark the ones that make light in your house.

For the Teacher: As the children color the pictures, name the different things that make light: lantern, sun, night light, flashlight, street light, lamp, car lights, candle. Talk about how the different lights are used. Help the children make a crayon mark on those lights that they use at home. You may want to bring several different lights or pictures of lights to show and discuss. Explain that we can be helpful lights to show God's love.

23

God's Loving Care
Matthew 6:25-34

Happy Bird Picture

Jesus wanted us to know that God will take care of us. Jesus told us to see how God takes care of birds. God gives birds trees for building their nests. He gives them wings to help them fly. Jesus said that God loves us much more than birds. God will take care of us, too.

Your teacher will help you make a beautiful bird to take home. You can glue a feather on your bird and add a twig under his feet for a resting place. Think of how God cares for you even more than He cares for beautiful birds.

For the Teacher: Provide a small twig, a small felt circle or moveable plastic eye, and a feather from a craft store or feather duster for each child. Let the children color their birds. Help each child glue a feather on the bird's wing, a felt circle or plastic eye on the eye, and a twig under the bird's feet. Talk about ways God cares for birds and ways He cares for us. Say a prayer of thanks.

Tipping Watering Can

Jesus talked about many things in our beautiful world that remind us of God's care.

Jesus told us to look at the wild flowers. They do not go to the store and buy petals. God sends sunshine and rain to make them bloom under His loving care.

You can care for flowers by giving them water. Your teacher will help you make a watering can and tip it toward the flowers. As you care for your picture garden, remember that God cares for you.

Finished Watering Can

God cares for me.

For the Teacher: Pre-cut a watering can and three flowers from brightly colored construction paper for each child. Give each child a sheet of green paper. Help them glue the flowers along the left side and bottom of the paper. Punch a hole through the center of the watering can. Help children attach the watering can above the flowers with a paper fastener. Cover the back of the paper fastener with tape. The children may turn the can to water the flowers.

The House on a Rock
Matthew 7:24-27

Build a House

Jesus told a story about two men who built houses. One man built a house on a rock. The other man built a house on the sand. When it rained, the house built on the rock stayed strong and safe inside. The house built on the sand fell down.

Like the house on the rock, God's love keeps you safe, too.

Your teacher will help you build a house on a rock. Color the house. You can glue black rocks to remind you of Jesus' story and cotton ball smoke to make the house warm.

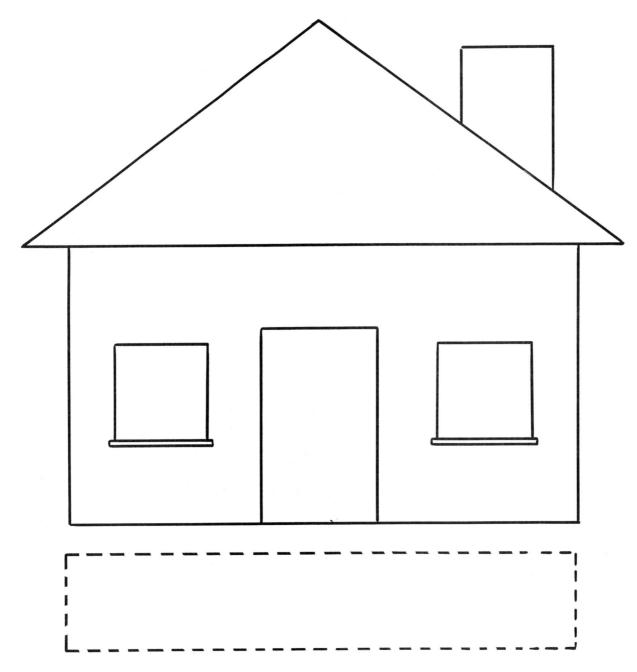

 For the Teacher: Duplicate the house pattern, one for each child. Also, cut out 1-inch black construction paper squares to represent rocks, five for each child. Cut two 1-inch yellow construction paper squares for each child as lights in the windows. Help the children glue on the rocks along the foundation, the lights in the windows, and add cotton balls above the chimney for smoke. Talk about how we can feel safe in our homes because Jesus is with us.

Make a Tool Set

Jesus said that a house built on a rock will be safe, even if it rains. This story tells us that God will take care of us if we love and obey Him.

Color the pictures to remind you of the house built on a rock. Your teacher will help you glue foil on the saw blade.

You can glue wood shavings around the tools. Can you name the tools? Which of them do you have at your home? Put a crayon mark on those you have seen.

Remember that God cares for you in your home. God wants you to love and obey Him.

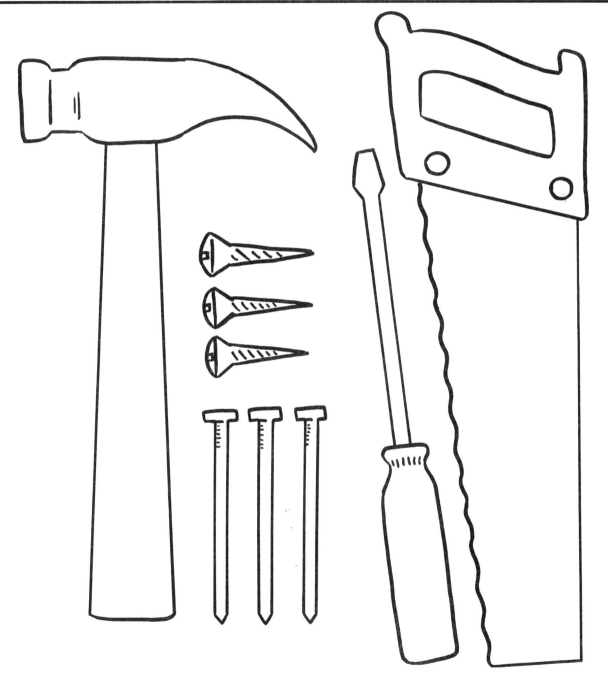

For the Teacher: Pre-cut aluminum foil pieces for saw blades, one for each child. Bring sawdust or wood shavings or 3/8 x 1-inch strips of paper, curled. After children color the pictures, help them glue foil to the saw blade. Dot glue around the tools and let children add wood shavings or sawdust. Talk about the ways we use each tool. Discuss ways God cares for us in our homes. Explain that Jesus worked with Joseph as a carpenter.

Jesus Blesses Children
Matthew 19:13-15

Jesus Loves Me Wristwatch

Some parents brought children to Jesus. They wanted Jesus to bless the children. His helpers said, "Jesus is too busy."

Jesus surprised them when He welcomed and blessed the boys and girls. Jesus always has time for children. He always has time for you.

You can make a Jesus Loves Me Wristwatch. Your teacher will help you make the wristwatch. The watch will help you remember that in daytime or nighttime Jesus always has time for you.

12

Jesus Always Has Time For Me

9

3

6

For the Teacher: Pre-cut a wristwatch and watch face for each child. As children color the watches, talk about the different times in a day. Ask the children to tell about their favorite times, such as play times, story times, and going to church times. Assure the children that Jesus always has time for them, any time of the day or night. Help children glue the faces on their watches. Staple the ends of the watch bands around their wrists.

28

Jesus Knows Picture

Jesus loves you and knows all about you. He watches over you all day long. Jesus watches over you in the night, too. He is your friend.

It feels good to know that Jesus is with you all the time. Even when you are sleeping, Jesus is there.

You can make a picture of some of the things Jesus knows about you. Your teacher will help you find your name and choose the colors to glue on your picture. You can add a cover to your picture. Lift the cover to see what Jesus knows about you.

Jesus knows:

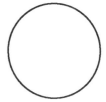

Glue cover here

- -

My name is:

My  **is:**

My 🏠 **is:**

I like ☀️ **days.**

For the Teacher: Pre-cut many 1-inch squares of colored construction paper, such as brown, black, yellow, red, blue, and white. Pre-cut small yellow circles for suns, one for each child. Also pre-cut a 6 x 9-inch piece of paper for each child. Print children's names on slips of paper, one name per paper. Help children glue their name, hair color, house color, and a yellow sun onto the picture. Then glue a paper cover on top. Fold it up for easy opening. 29

The Good Farmer
Mark 4:3-9

Muffin Paper Flower Garden

Jesus told a story about a farmer to teach us to listen to God's Word, the Bible. The good farmer walked around his farm. He planted many seeds. When the seed fell on good soil, many plants grew. When we listen to God's Word, we grow, too.

You can make a garden. Your teacher will help you glue green stems and leaves for your garden. Your teacher will show you how to add muffin paper flowers to the stems. You can thank Jesus for teaching you how to listen to God's Word.

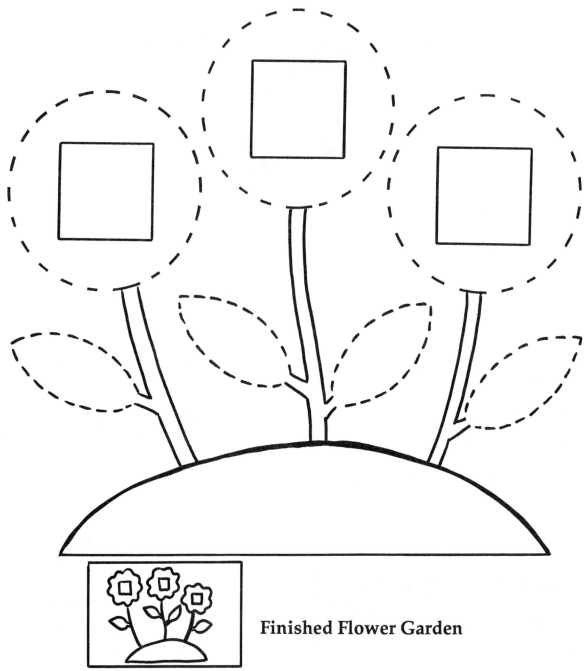

Finished Flower Garden

For the Teacher: Pre-cut five or six leaves and three 1-inch squares from bright paper for each child. Place two muffin papers inside each other, and make three blossoms for each child. Give each child a sheet of blue construction paper. Help them glue this pattern page onto the blue paper and then glue three green chenille wires on the picture for stems. Let them add leaves and blossoms to the stems and glue a square on each blossom.

Grow a Crop

Jesus said that we should learn about Him by listening to God's Word, the Bible. As we listen to Bible stories about Jesus, we grow to love Him more and more.

God is the Good Farmer Who helps us grow. You can grow plants like a farmer.

Your teacher will show you how to prepare the soil, plant the seeds, and water them. Soon you will see beautiful plants grow, just like a farmer. Once your plants have sprouted, you can take them home to watch them grow.

Grow in grace.
— 2 Peter 3:18

Finished Crop

 For the Teacher: Provide a small plastic container, a pre-cut farmer and a scripture card for each child. Add the child's name to the farmer's bib. Help the children fill the containers with planter mix to within one inch of the top. Scatter wheatberry seeds or lima beans on top. Cover the seeds with more mix and sprinkle water to dampen. Tape a scripture and a farmer to each container, as shown. Keep seeds moist and in sunlight for two weeks.

The Best Rule
Mark 12:28-31

My Loving Hand Print

One day some people asked Jesus what God wants us to do. Jesus told them that, first of all, God wants us to love Him. Second, Jesus said, God wants us to love each other.

We can show we love God by going to church, talking to Him in prayer, and loving God's Word, the Bible. We can show we love others by being helpful and kind.

Sometimes we use our hands to help other people. Your teacher will help you make a picture of your own hand print to take home. God gave you a special hand print.

Finished Hand Print

For the Teacher: Pre-cut a white circle pattern for each child. Write the date and child's name, as shown. Fold a sheet of bright construction paper in half to make a 6 x 9-inch stand-up sheet for each child. Keep moist towels and smocks at hand. Place the child's hand into a small amount of poster paint, then on the circle (or trace the hand print). Help each child glue the circle (when dry) to the folded paper, as shown. Provide extra paper for practicing.

The Best Rule Medallion

Jesus said that God is pleased and happy when we love Him. God is pleased and happy when we love others, too. Jesus called this the best rule, because loving God and others pleases God most of all.

You can love God and others by being kind.

Your teacher will help you make a Best Rule Medallion to wear. You can wear the medallion home. The medallion will tell people that you want to make God happy by loving Him and loving others.

I LOVE GOD

Taped Loop

Folded Blue Ribbon

For the Teacher: Provide a white "I Love God" circle, a 4-inch blue poster board circle, and a 3 1/4-inch circle of gold foil for each child. Each child will also need a blue paper strip, folded as shown, and a 9-inch piece of narrow gold ribbon. Help the children glue the gold circle on the blue one and then glue the white circle on top. Glue the folded blue "ribbon" to the back. Loop the gold ribbon and tape to the top of the medallion. Safety pin on clothing. 33

Jesus Calms the Sea
Luke 8:22-25

Beautiful Day Texture Picture

One day Jesus took a boat trip with His helpers. They enjoyed sailing in boats. They liked the blue water and the gentle waves.

Jesus took a nap. When the winds began to blow, the waves grew big. Jesus' helpers felt afraid. They woke Jesus.

Jesus made the water smooth again. That made everyone happy. The helpers were thankful that Jesus was with them.

Your teacher will help you make a special picture to remind you of that beautiful day.

 For the Teacher: Give each child a sheet of bright blue construction paper, a dark blue crayon, a pre-cut 1-inch yellow circle, cotton balls, colored spiral macaroni for boats, and a small piece of sandpaper for the beach. Show the children a sample lake picture. Have them color the lake. Help them glue their papers to the construction paper background and paste the sun, clouds, boats, and beach on their picture.

Make a Sailor Hat

After Jesus calmed the sea, the water was smooth once again. His helpers were very glad that Jesus was with them.

Jesus is with us, just as He was with His helpers in the boat. Jesus walks with us. Jesus rides with us. Jesus is always near.

Your teacher will help you make a sailor hat. You can glue a sign on your hat that says, "Jesus sails with me." The hat will help you remember that Jesus is with you all the time. You can say, "Thank You, Jesus, for being with me."

Fold construction paper or 1/4 newspaper sheet:

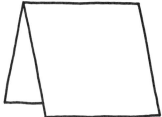

1. Fold top corners to center.

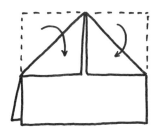

2. Fold bottom lip up, on each side.

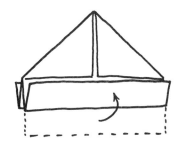

3. Fold bottom up again.

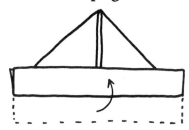

4. Open at bottom and place on child's head.

Jesus Sails With Me.

For the Teacher: Pre-cut a "Jesus Sails With Me" sign for each child. Let children color the signs. Make a sailor hat from newspaper or construction paper for each child, as shown. Help children glue the sign to their hat. Talk about the fact that Jesus is always with us. Lead the children in a prayer of thanks.

The Good Samaritan
Luke 10:25-37

Helping Others Picture

Jesus told a story about a good man who lived in Samaria. He was called a Samaritan. The good Samaritan stopped to help a hurt man beside the road. He wrapped the hurt man in bandages and found him a place to stay. Jesus wants us to be kind and help others like the Good Samaritan.

Pretend to be the kind man. Glue a cotton ball pillow under the hurt man's head. Put a bandage on his hurt leg.

Think of some ways you can help other people this week.

 For the Teacher: Provide a cotton ball and a small adhesive bandage for each child. Help children glue a cotton ball under the hurt man's head for a pillow and attach an adhesive bandage to his leg. Talk with them about ways to be kind and helpful to friends and family members.

Be Kind Poster

The Good Samaritan story teaches us to be kind and help others. There are many ways we can be kind. At home we can pick up our toys, help set the table, and be gentle with our pets. At church we can take turns, share toys, and listen when the teacher is talking.

Can you think of other ways to be kind? Jesus is happy when we are kind, like the good Samaritan, who stopped to help the hurt man.

You can make a colorful Be Kind Poster. The poster will remind you to be kind to others.

 For the Teacher: After the children color, help them glue their pictures on bright construction paper. Tape a yarn hanger on the back. Talk about ways the children can be kind and helpful to others.

37

We Can Talk to God
Luke 11:1-10

Jesus talked to God often in prayer. Jesus wants us to talk to God, too. We can talk to God any time and anywhere. We can talk to God about anything. God wants us to talk to Him every day. We talk to God when we pray. We can pray any time and anywhere.

Talking to God

Color the pictures. Which ones do you like to talk to God about? Choose one picture that you especially enjoy. Your teacher will help you talk to God about that picture.

You can talk to God at home or at church or anywhere you are.

For the Teacher: Talk about the pictures as the children color them. Discuss different prayers each picture might represent. For instance, the friends picture might be, "Thank you for my friend," or "Help me share my toys with my friend." Help children choose one picture they want to talk to God about (pets, home, friends, or family). Gently encourage each child to say a simple sentence prayer with your assistance.

Jesus Hears Me Plaque

When we talk to God in prayer, He listens and hears what we say. He is always awake. He is always with us. He is always waiting to hear our prayers.

You can make a beautiful plaque to hang in your room.

Color the picture. Your teacher will help you glue your picture to a paper plate and add bright macaroni around the border. You can add a yarn tie. Then you can take your plaque home and hang it on the wall.

Jesus hears me

Finished Plaque

For the Teacher: Pre-cut a "Jesus Hears Me" circle for each child to color. Provide a 9-inch paper plate for each child. Punch two holes near the top. Help children glue the colored circle in the center. Spread glue around the edge of the picture so they can add a circle of colored macaroni around it. Give each child a 12-inch piece of yarn and help them thread it through the holes. Tie a bow so they can hang the plaque at home.

The Lost Coin
Luke 15:8-10

Hidden Coin Picture

Jesus told a story about a woman who had ten coins. One day she lost one of her coins. She looked and looked for the coin. The woman looked everywhere to find the lost coin.

Jesus said that God loves you even more than the woman loved her lost coin.

Color the picture. Then help the woman find her lost coin. Your teacher will give you a coin to glue on the table where the woman can see it. Draw a smile on the woman's face.

Your teacher will help you thank God for loving you so much.

For the Teacher: Pre-cut a 1-inch circle from aluminum foil for each child. Let the children color the picture and glue the lost coin on the table. Show them how to draw a smile on the woman's face. Help them count to ten on their fingers to understand how many coins the woman had. Say a prayer, "Thank You, God, for loving us so much. Thank You, God, for loving us even more than the woman loved her lost coin."

Make a Treasure Box

The Lost Coin
Luke 15:8-10

Jesus told a story about a woman who looked and looked to find her lost coin. The woman was so happy when she found the coin that she called her friends to have a party. Jesus told the story to show that God is happy, too, when we love and obey Him.

Color your coin box and attach a handle. Your teacher will give you some foil coins to put inside your box. Just like the woman who found her coin, God is happy when you obey Him.

Handle

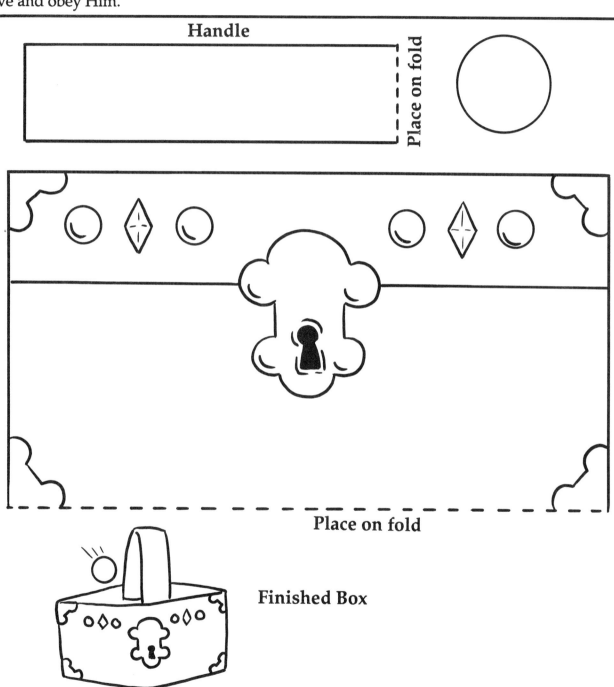

Place on fold

Place on fold

Finished Box

For the Teacher: Pre-cut ten 1-inch circles from aluminum foil or gift wrap for each child. Duplicate a coin box for each child. Place the box pattern on a folded piece of construction paper and cut it apart. After the children have colored their boxes, tape the sides and attach a paper handle. (Leave the top of the coin box open.) Help the children place the coins into their boxes.

 **Jesus Heals a Blind Man**
Luke 18:35-43

Happy Day Picture

The blind man sat by the road. He could not see pretty flowers. He could not see smiling faces. His world was dark.

Jesus came by and healed the blind man. Now he could see Jesus' face. What a happy day this was for the blind man.

The blind man thanked Jesus for helping him see. You can thank Jesus for helping you, too.

Make your own Happy Day Picture. Glue a picture of Jesus onto the black circle. Your teacher will help you add a handle.

Thank You, Jesus, for helping me.

 For the Teacher: Make a copy of the Happy Day circle for each child. Cut a black circle of construction paper the same size, one for each child. Help children attach a tongue depressor handle to the black circle, using tape or glue. Let children glue yarn on the picture of Jesus for hair and a beard. Glue the black circles to the backs of the pictures of Jesus. Let children turn their pictures from "blind" to "seeing." Say a prayer of thanks.

Beautiful Butterfly

What a happy day this was for the blind man. Now he could see trees and grass. He could see smiling faces. He could see colorful butterflies. The man looked up at the blue sky. He looked up at the bright sun. He thanked God that Jesus helped him to see.

We can thank God for our beautiful world, too. Your teacher will help you make a colorful butterfly. The butterfly can help remind you to thank God for the wonderful things He has created.

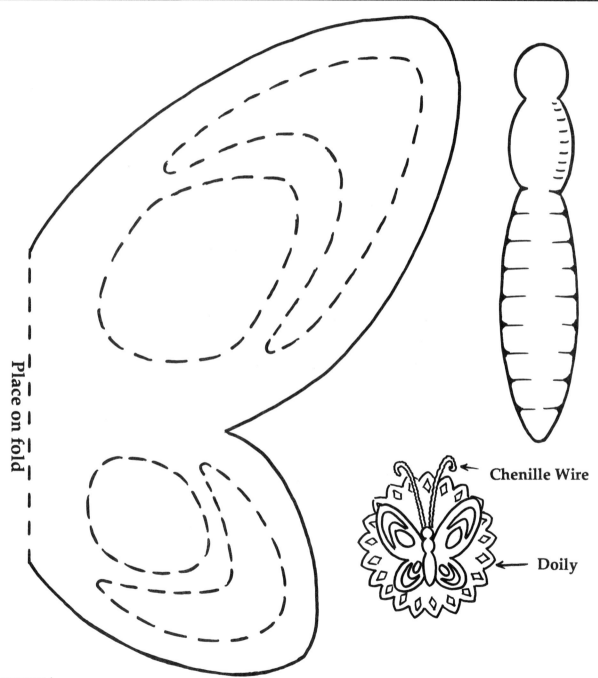

Place on fold

Chenille Wire

Doily

For the Teacher: Provide a 10-inch or 12-inch paper doily for each child. Pre-cut a butterfly from yellow paper. Pre-cut spots and a body from green or purple paper for each child, using the patterns. Show children how to bend chenille wires to make antennae, as shown. Attach antennae to the butterfly with tape. Help children glue the body and the wing spots onto the butterfly wings. Then, help each child glue the butterfly onto a paper doily.

43

Zaccheus and Jesus
Luke 19:1-10

Meeting Jesus Picture

"I hope I can see Jesus," Zaccheus said, as he huffed and puffed up a tree and perched on a branch. Zaccheus was too short to stand by the road when Jesus passed by. All he could see there were people, people, people.

As Jesus drew near, He looked up and saw Zaccheus. He called out his name! "Zaccheus, hurry down right now! I'm coming to your house today!"

Color the picture. Your teacher will help you add Jesus' arm so He can wave to Zaccheus.

For the Teacher: Pre-cut a picture of Jesus' arm for each child. After the children color, help them attach the arm at the black dot with a paper fastener. Place tape over the back of the paper fastener to avoid scratching. You may want to have each child glue the completed page to a piece of bright construction paper for reinforcement. One at a time, substitute the children's names as you say Jesus' words to Zaccheus.

44

Obeying Jesus

Jesus looked up when He came to Zacchaeus in the tree. "Come down!" He called. "I'm coming to your house!"

Zacchaeus had not been obeying God before he met Jesus. He quickly decided to love and obey God with all his heart.

Color your picture of Jesus visiting in Zacchaeus' home. Your teacher will help you glue food onto the plates. Draw a smile on Zacchaeus. Say a prayer of thanks to Jesus for loving each of us so much.

For the Teacher: Provide raisins, croutons, small fish crackers, and cereal circles for the children to glue on their pictures. Help those who need assistance to draw a smile on Zacchaeus. Talk about how happy Zacchaeus was when he decided to obey Jesus. Think of ways that children can obey at home: picking up toys, giving hugs to parents, being kind to friends. Say a prayer thanking Jesus for loving each of us so much.

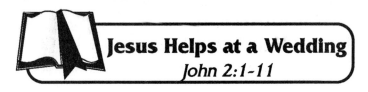

Jesus Helps at a Wedding
John 2:1-11

A Happy Wedding Picture

Jesus went to a wedding one day. At the party, the people became sad when there was nothing left to drink. Jesus asked the servants to go and get enough water to fill six big jars. Then Jesus turned the water into a new and better drink. The people at the wedding were very happy.

Color the picture of the wedding. Your teacher will help you fill the water jugs. You can clap your hands to thank Jesus for making the wedding happy again.

 For the Teacher: Pre-cut six blue circles from construction paper for each child. Let children color their pictures. Then spread glue on top of the jars in the picture. Let the children add the blue circles to fill the jars with water. You may serve a small cup of juice to each child. Have the children say, "Thank You, Jesus," as they clap their hands.

Jesus Helps Me Banner

One day some people asked Jesus to use His special power to help them at a wedding. After Jesus helped them, the people were very happy.

Color the pictures of the sad boy, the happy girl, and Jesus, Who is ready to help them.

Make a banner to remind you that in sad times or in happy times, Jesus helps you, too. Glue the circles on the paper ribbon. Your teacher will show you how to make a hanger for your banner.

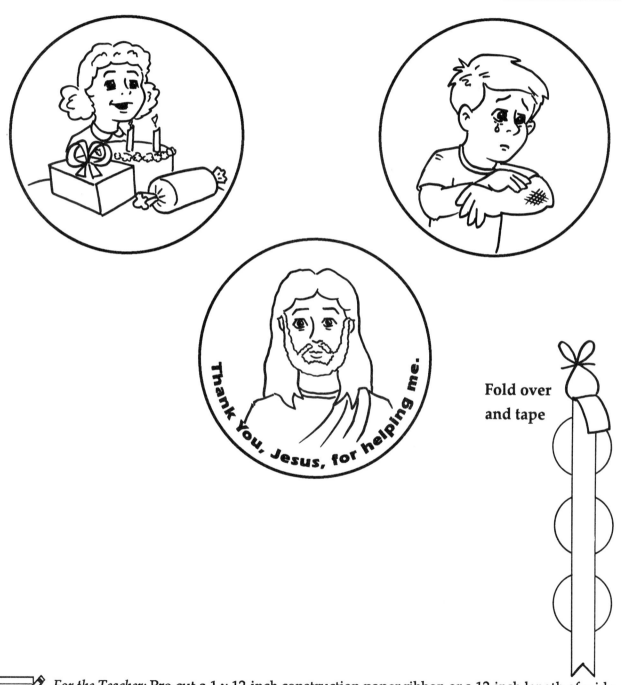

Fold over and tape

Thank You, Jesus, for helping me.

For the Teacher: Pre-cut a 1 x 12-inch construction paper ribbon or a 12-inch length of wide ribbon for each child. Pre-cut the three circle patterns and give one set to each child to color. Help the children glue their circles on the ribbon. Fold the top of each ribbon down 1 inch and place a piece of yarn through the fold. Tape the top down securely over the yarn. Tie the yarn in a bow to make a hanger. Talk about the sad or happy times when Jesus helps us. 47

Jesus Feeds a Crowd
John 6:5-14

Picnic People Stick Puppets

Many people came to hear Jesus and see His miracles. One day, as Jesus talked, the people got hungry. A boy gave Jesus his lunch of five small rolls and two little fish. Jesus used the boy's small lunch to feed over 5,000 people. The people knew Jesus was God's Son.

Color the pictures. Your teacher will cut out the pictures and show you how to make the boy and Jesus into stick puppets. Your teacher will help you tape a handle on your basket. You can pass the basket from the boy to Jesus.

Tape ribbon handle to basket.

For the Teacher: Cut apart the puppets and picnic basket after the children color them. Help children glue each figure to a tongue depressor to make a puppet. Tape both ends of a 3-inch piece of ribbon to each basket top so the child can pass the picnic lunch from the boy's hand to Jesus. Show the children how to move the child close to Jesus so he can receive a hug.

A Picnic Time Basket

The little boy was happy to share his picnic lunch with Jesus. The boy gave Jesus a small gift of five rolls and two fish. Jesus made the boy's lunch into a big gift to feed many people.

You can make a picnic basket to help you remember the story of the boy's picnic lunch.

Your teacher will show you how to add a handle to the picnic basket and put a pretty napkin inside. Then your teacher will help you put five loaves and two fish in your picnic basket for lunch.

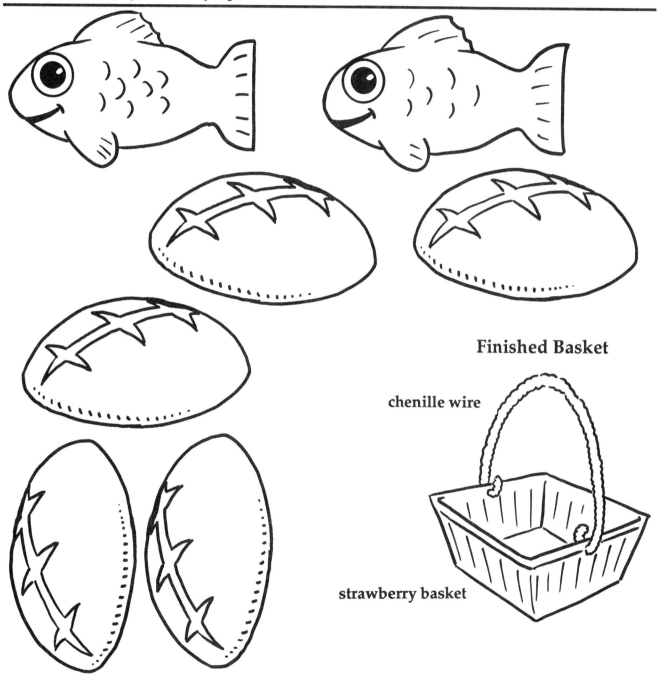

Finished Basket

chenille wire

strawberry basket

For the Teacher: Provide each child with a small plastic basket, such as is used for cherry tomatoes or berries. Cut two fish and five rolls out of construction paper for each child. Help the children twist chenille wire handles onto their baskets. Let each child put a napkin in his basket. Help children add the fish and rolls. Say "thank You" to God together for giving us everything we need.

The Good Shepherd
John 10:11

Shepherd Texture Picture

There were many sheep in the land where Jesus lived. Shepherds took care of the sheep. The shepherds kept the sheep safe and fed them.

Jesus is the Good Shepherd. He cares for us. Jesus helps keep us safe and provides us with the food we eat.

Color the Good Shepherd picture. Your teacher will help you glue a chenille wire for the shepherd's staff. Then your teacher will show you how to glue on fringed grass and cotton ball sheep.

For the Teacher: After the children have colored their pictures, give them chenille wires and cotton balls. Provide bits of green construction paper grass, Easter grass, or real grass. Show them how to glue the chenille wire staff on the shepherd's arm, a cotton ball sheep in his other arm, sheep by his side, and grass by the stream. Talk about how a shepherd cares for his sheep, just as Jesus cares for us.

Make a Marshmallow Lamb

A shepherd knows the name of each of his sheep and lambs. He takes care of the sheep each day. He takes care of the lambs, too.

Jesus is the Good Shepherd. You are His little lamb. Jesus knows your name. Jesus takes care of you.

You can make a marshmallow lamb. Your teacher will help you glue your lamb picture onto construction paper. Then your teacher will help you glue fluffy marshmallows to cover your lamb. You can say, "I am Jesus' little lamb."

Finished Lamb

I Am Jesus' Little Lamb

For the Teacher: Pre-cut a lamb picture and "Jesus' Little Lamb" sign for each child. Provide 25-30 mini-marshmallows, one 9 x 6-inch piece of green construction paper, and a tiny bow for each child. Help each child glue the lamb and sign on the paper. Spread glue over the lamb, and show the child how to cover it with marshmallows. Add a bow and the child's name. Bend the sides of the paper forward to make the marshmallow lamb stand up. 51

A Family Jesus Loved
John 11:1-45

Jesus' Special Friends Picture

Jesus had a family He loved to visit. The members of the family were Mary, Martha, and Lazarus. Jesus ate with them in their home. Jesus talked with them in their home. Mary, Martha, Lazarus, and Jesus were all special friends.

You can help Jesus' friends get ready for Jesus to visit their home. Color the pictures. Your teacher will help you glue a bowl of flowers on the table. You can glue food on the plates. You can get ready for Jesus' visit.

For the Teacher: Cut out a flower picture for each child. Provide bowls of raisins, fish crackers, croutons, and cereal circles for the children to glue on their pictures. Bring extra food for sampling. Talk about how we can make our home a welcome place for Jesus.

Sad to Happy Picture

Mary and Martha were very sad. Their brother Lazarus had become very sick and died. When Jesus arrived, He made Lazarus alive again. This was a wonderful miracle for Jesus' good friends. Mary, Martha, and Lazarus were very happy.

Color the picture. Your teacher will show you how to make Lazarus return to his sisters. You can draw smiles on Mary, Martha, and Lazarus to give them happy faces. What do you think the family may have said to Jesus for doing this special thing?

Finished Picture

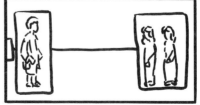

For the Teacher: Pre-cut the pictures. Place tape at the top and bottom of a 1 x 3-inch strip of paper. Attach a strip vertically on the back of each Lazarus picture. Give each child a 10-inch piece of yarn. Tape one end of the yarn onto a sheet of blue paper. Help children color Mary and Martha and glue them on the taped end of the yarn. Insert the loose end of yarn through the strip behind Lazarus and tape it to the blue paper. Move him to his sisters and add smiles. 53

TEACHING ACTIVITIES

Jesus' Life & Ministry

Follow Me (Pages 20 and 21)

Play a game of "Simon Says." Remind children that Jesus asks us to follow Him in our actions and kind words.

The Lighted Candle (Pages 22 and 23)

Bring a tape player and music cassette. After making a **Shining Bright Candle,** pass the candle around the circle of children, as music plays. When music stops, the child with the candle stands up, as you say, "Gretchen, let your light shine," and then name something Gretchen can do to be kind and loving (help parents, share a toy, etc.). Continue until each child has had a turn.

God's Loving Care (Pages 24 and 25)
The House on a Rock (Pages 26 and 27)

As they make the **Happy Bird Picture, Tipping Watering Can, House on a Rock,** and **Tool Set,** tell the children that God loves them and they are special. Say, "God cares for you, Jason. Your smile (or helpfulness, kindness, etc.) is very special."

Jesus Blesses Children (Pages 28 and 29)

Have children say, "Jesus loves me" together. Then have children sit in a circle. Hand one child a ball or bean bag and help that child say, "Jesus loves me." That child may hand it to another. Continue until each child has had at least one turn.

The Good Farmer (Pages 30 and 31)
The Best Rule (Pages 32 and 33)

Explain that God loves us and helps us grow. God is happy when we love Him. God is pleased when we love others. Encourage children to show their love by sharing a toy or a crayon with others. Say, "Jennifer, thank you for sharing."

Jesus Calms the Sea (Pages 34 and 35)
The Good Samaritan (Pages 36 and 37)

Enlarge the **Helping Others Picture** pattern, add cuts to the hurt man, and tape the picture to a wall. Have children stand at the opposite end of the room. Give the first child an open adhesive bandage. Have that child run to the wall and put it on the hurt man.

We Can Talk to God (Pages 38 and 39)
The Lost Coin (Pages 40 and 41)

Make extra foil coins, several for each child. Hide them around the room and let children go on a treasure hunt to find them. Help any children who cannot locate coins.

Jesus Heals a Blind Man (Pages 42 and 43)
Zacchaeus and Jesus (Pages 44 and 45)

Tell the story of Zacchaeus from Luke 19: 1-10 after children make the **Meeting Jesus Picture.** Prompt children to move Jesus' arm as He sees Zacchaeus and asks him to come down. Use the picture of Jesus to tell the story of the blind man.

Jesus Helps at a Wedding (Pages 46 and 47)
Jesus Feeds a Crowd (Pages 48 and 49)

After children make **Picnic People Stick Puppets,** retell the stories from John 2:1-11 or John 6:5-14. Prompt children to hold up the Jesus puppet whenever you mention Jesus. Eventually add the boy puppet for the story, **Jesus Feeds a Crowd.**

The Good Shepherd (Pages 50 and 51)
A Family Jesus Loved (Pages 52 and 53)

Explain that Jesus cared for Mary, Martha, and Lazarus, and Jesus takes care of each child. Lead children in singing, "Jesus Loves Me, This I Know."

BIBLE STORIES ABOUT JESUS

Activities for Ages 2 & 3

Jesus' Death & Resurrection

The People Praise Jesus
Matthew 21:1-11

Praise Parade Texture Picture

Jesus made many people well. He made the sea calm. He told people that God loves them.

When Jesus rode into Jerusalem on a donkey, the people had a parade for Him. They laid coats and palm branches in His path to show Jesus that they loved Him.

The people sang praise songs to Jesus, God's Son.

Color the picture of Jesus riding into Jerusalem. Your teacher will help you glue coats and palm branches in the path. You can praise Jesus for being your friend.

For the Teacher: Provide small real or artificial leaves or ferns and bits of cloth for the praise parade picture. After children have colored, show them how to glue the leaves and pieces of cloth on the path. They may also glue leaves in people's hands. The children may enjoy using towels and large branches to make a path in the classroom and sing a praise song to Jesus.

Joyful Praise Tambourine

The people were so happy to see Jesus. They were excited that He was God's Son. The people were glad that Jesus was coming to Jerusalem. They shouted and sang for joy. The people praised Jesus for being God's Son. They sang songs of gladness.

Color the circle. Your teacher will help you glue it on your tambourine. You can decorate it with ribbon. Your teacher will help you finish your tambourine. Then you and your friends can have a praise parade together.

Finished Tambourine

For the Teacher: For each child you will need an empty margarine or whipped topping container; rice, coarse cereal, or small rocks; and several strips of pastel and foil ribbon about eighteen inches long. After the children color their circles, help glue them to the container lids. Add the rice, cereal, or rocks. Place the ends of ribbon inside the container and close the lid, making streamers. Tape the lid shut. Lead children in a parade.

Jesus Serves Supper
Luke 22:8-20

Make a Meal Picture

Jesus wanted to eat a special meal with His helpers. Jesus told the helpers what to do to get ready for the meal. Jesus told the helpers how to find the room where they would eat. The helpers obeyed Jesus. The helpers found a large room and got it ready for their meal with Jesus.

You can help get ready for Jesus' special supper. Color the pictures of delicious food. Your teacher will help you cut the pictures apart and glue them on a paper plate to serve at Jesus' special supper.

Non-Edible Play Clay Recipe
Combine 2 1/2 cups flour, 1/2 cup salt, 1 3/4 cups boiling water and 2 teaspoons vegetable oil. Turn out on a flat surface and knead until smooth. Store in airtight containers at room temperature.

For the Teacher: Give each child a paper plate. After they color, help them cut out food and glue it on the plates. Make non-edible play clay. Combine 2 1/2 cups flour, 1/2 cup salt, 1 3/4 cups boiling water and 2 teaspoons vegetable oil. Knead until smooth. Store in airtight containers. Let children mold the clay into food shapes and glue it on their plates. Remind them not to eat the clay. Tape a recipe to each plate and cover plates with foil.

Make and Serve Supper

Jesus told His helpers that He wanted to share a special supper with them. They ate and talked together. His helpers knew that Jesus loved them.

We will prepare a special supper to eat now. Color your placemat. Then you can help make the sandwiches. You can help set the table for the special supper.

Special Sandwich Filling: Mix together 1 cup peanut butter, 1/4 cup chopped raisins, 2 tablespoons honey, and 1 tablespoon orange juice.

For the Teacher: After children color placemats, make the sandwich filling (or serve grape halves and cheese). Let children add ingredients as you mix. Spread filling on bread and cut into tiny sandwiches. Do not let children touch sharp utensils. Give everyone a small job. The children may put colorful napkins, cups, and placemats on the table. (Later, you may fill the cups with water or juice.) They may add streamers or a centerpiece.

Easter's Glad Story
Mark 15:25-27, 39; 16:1-6

Easter Cross Decoration

Jesus died on the cross, but He did not stay dead. He became alive again in three days, just as He had said He would.

The picture of a cross reminds us of how much Jesus loves us. You can make an Easter cross decoration to put in your home.

Your teacher will show you how to cover your cross with sandpaper and make it stand up in a play clay base. Then your teacher will show you how to make flowers grow around the bottom of the cross.

Jesus Loves Me.

For the Teacher: Pre-cut a sandpaper cross and a cardboard cross for each child. Help the children glue the sandpaper cross to the cardboard. Show them how to press the cross into a large play clay base. Provide small artificial flowers and leaves or construction paper flowers taped to green chenille wire for the children to press into the clay base.

Happy Sponge Paintings

When Jesus became alive again, His helpers were very happy. They wanted everyone to hear the good news.

Springtime reminds us of Easter joy. Warm weather returns, flowers begin to grow, and new animal babies are born.

You can make a sponge painting to help you remember that Jesus is alive. Your teacher will help you create beautiful designs with the sponges. You can be happy that Jesus is alive. You can thank God for Jesus.

For the Teacher: Provide small bath sponges of baby animals, such as chicks or bunnies, or cut small oval sponges in half to make caterpillars, butterflies, and bugs. A small piece of a regular sponge also may be used. Clip a spring-type clothespin to the sponge for a handle. Provide poster paints in springtime colors. Let children put dampened sponges in a small amount of paint, then on paper. They may practice on scrap paper.

61

Jesus' Special Promise
Matthew 28:18-20

Jesus gave His helpers a special promise before He went back to heaven. Jesus promised that He would always be with them.

Jesus promised to be with you always, too. He is with you when you play outside. He is with you at home. Jesus is with you at church.

"I Am With You" Picture

You can make a picture of Jesus to remember that Jesus is always with you. Your teacher will help you glue a piece of cloth onto Jesus' robe. You can add your picture to show Jesus holding you in His arms.

I am with you, _____.

Glue photo here.

 For the Teacher: Take an instant photo of each child. Give each child a piece of soft colorful fabric and a picture of Jesus. Help children glue the fabric to Jesus' robe. Spread glue on Jesus' arm and let each child attach a photo. Add the child's name to the picture. Talk about Jesus' special promise to be with us always.

Promise Holder

Jesus came to earth to give us joy and love. He gave us a special promise to be with us always. We can be happy that Jesus loves us so much.

You can make a Promise Holder to remember that Jesus is always with you.

You can color the pictures and glue them to paper strips. Your teacher will help you staple the holder to a paper plate. Then you can arrange the pictures so that they peek out of your promise holder.

Jesus is with me.

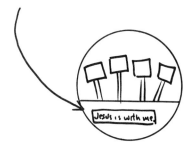

For the Teacher: Provide a whole and a half 7-inch paper plate for each child. Cut six 6 x 1/2-inch construction paper strips for each child. After children color the pictures, cut the pictures apart and help them glue each picture to a paper strip. Also help them staple the half plate to the whole one. Show the children how to make their promise pictures peek over the side of the holder. Talk about the pictures. Thank Jesus for always being with us.

TEACHING ACTIVITIES

Jesus' Death & Resurrection

The People Praise Jesus (Pages 56 and 57)

Tell about Jesus' triumphal entry into Jerusalem from Matthew 21:1-11. Talk about how we feel when we see a parade. Help children understand how people must have felt to see Jesus.

Joyful Praise Tambourine: Bring a tape player and music cassette or invite someone to play the piano. After children make their tambourines, show them how to shake the tambourines to make noise. As the music plays, lead the children in a parade around the room. If they know the song, encourage them to sing along. If other instruments are available, let children take turns playing them, too.

Jesus Serves Supper (Pages 58 and 59)

Talk about Jesus' last supper with His disciples (helpers) from Luke 22:8-20. Explain that Jesus wanted to eat a meal with His friends to remind the friends that He loved them.

Make and Serve Supper: Before eating, cover each child's placemat with waxed paper or plastic wrap. As children eat, talk about how much Jesus loves each of them. After the meal is finished, encourage children to help with the clean up. They can throw away their plates, napkins, and cups.

They may take their placemats home, after tossing dirty waxed paper or plastic wrap.

Easter's Glad Story (Pages 60 and 61)

Tell the story of Jesus' death and resurrection from Mark 15:25-27, 39 and Mark 16:1-6. Remind children that Jesus loves them very much.

Easter Cross Decoration: As children make their crosses, lead them in singing a joyful song or play some happy music. When the crosses are completed, explain that they remind us of Jesus' love. Prompt children to say together, "Jesus loves me." Say a prayer of thanks to Jesus for His love.

Jesus' Special Promise (Pages 62 and 63)

Talk about Jesus' special promise to be with His helpers always. Explain that Jesus is with us always, too. Name different times and places when Jesus is with the children.

Promise Holder: After making the holder, play a Promise Game. Have children take turns choosing a promise from their holder, standing, and holding it up for all to see. Say a few words about the picture. Then say, "Jesus promises to be with us when we play" (or when we're unhappy, when it rains, etc.). Continue until each child has had at least one turn.